Contents

facing life's trials together

I see padlocks. Thousands of them. They are clasped to the rails of the Pont des Arts bridge in Paris. Their brass cases hang along the walkway like the yellow leaves of autumn — leaves one hopes will never fall.

The reason for the locks is quaint. Sweethearts meet on the bridge, write their names on a padlock, weave its hook through the wire mesh of the bridge's fence, and lock it tight. Then, as the sun sets over the city, the couple take the key and throw it into the Seine as a symbolic gesture of their eternal love. These locks reveal the longing each of us has to be clasped and bonded to someone who will be with us to the end.

Merryn and I are in Paris to celebrate our 15th wedding anniversary. It's a significant event for us. Just a few months ago we ended the most difficult chapter of our lives. After a decade spent trying everything to start a family — from special diets, healing prayer and numerous rounds of in-vitro fertilisation, to an agonising two-year wait on an Australian adoption list — we brought our dream of having a child to an end and moved to England to start again. We are

starting life over. This is our 'resurrection year'.

"Happy anniversary," I say to Merryn, as we sit in a Montmartre restaurant after visiting the Pont des Arts and other Paris sights.

"15 years and never a cross word," she jokes.

Like any couple, we've had our conflicts, but never more so than during the last 10 years. Infertility

These locks reveal the longing each of us has to be clasped and bonded to someone who will be with us to the end.

forced us to wrestle with questions and decisions we'd never expected to face. On many occasions we disagreed on the path forward, and spent long hours getting to a point of sacrifice or compromise.

"Remember our first flat?" I say, reminiscing on earlier, easier times. "Remember the secondhand couches and the borrowed TV?"

"And remember when we moved to Perth?" Merryn says. "We left home and proved we could make it on our own."

"Perhaps that's when we really became a couple," I say. "That's when we started facing crises and learned to walk through them together."

I top up our champagne and we hold hands across the table, breaking only when the waitress arrives with our meals. Another memory floats to mind as we talk and eat. It's from a while back, when we first started wondering if IVF was worth a try.

"In-vitro fertilisation can strain a relationship," the counsellor had told us, as we sat in a discussion room at the hospital.

"We've heard the drugs can cause emotional upsets for the woman," I said. "Is that what you mean?"

"Not just that," she replied. "You'll have many decisions to make if you go ahead, like how many rounds of IVF you'll attempt and what you'll do if you don't succeed. It can lead to disagreements."

"We've talked about that," Merryn said, "and we've decided we won't let IVF come between us. Our marriage is more important than having a child."

With that the counsellor slumped with relief and dropped her objective social worker stance. "I'm so glad you said that," she said. "Only last week a woman told me in front of her husband that if she didn't have a baby, their marriage was through."

Our marriage is more important than having a child. In hindsight, it was this

"Perhaps that's when we really became a couple," I say. "That's when we started facing crises and learned to walk through them together."

> 66
>
> *Our marriage is more important than having a child. In hindsight, it was this commitment that saved us through the trials and tears.*

commitment that saved us through the trials and tears of the years that followed. From making a home to moving cities to facing crises, we decided to let nothing come between us.

Sadly, some of those autumn leaves on the Pont des Arts bridge do fall. Some couples retrieve the key and set themselves free from their 'eternal'

love. Others are prised apart by a lover, a career, or the pursuit of a child at any cost. We understand that pressure now.

But some padlocks go unbroken, the key long forgotten, competing forces withstood. A little weathered from the storms and tarnished in places, they remain locked, clasped, bonded, wedded.

Sheridan Voysey

Sheridan is a writer, speaker and broadcaster, frequently contributing to BBC Radio 2's Pause for Thought. His books include *Resurrection Year: Turning Broken Dreams into New Beginnings*, which recounts how he and his wife started again after a decade of infertility.

understanding one another

When you get married there's a lot of talk of two becoming one, and union and partnership.
All of that is great and right, but one of the things Steve and I have learned in our marriage is the importance of knowing who we are as individuals, in the midst of the oneness.

It's knowing what we each bring to the partnership – our gifts, talents, hobbies and quirks. Those things have morphed and changed over time. Steve has discovered the joys of a lazy lie-in on a Saturday morning, and I have come to appreciate a good curry. Some things, however, remain the same – the theme tune to Match Of The Day (MOTD) still triggers a disproportionate level of annoyance in me and Steve has never developed an enjoyment of mooching around the shops. So we don't do those things together. We still do them, but we do them alone or with other people.

In fact, MOTD was really what started our journey to understanding our individual needs and likes. Who knew it could have such a positive effect? Steve travels a lot at weekends and often gets home late in the evening. When we were first married, this led to some misunderstandings – but not the type you might expect.

Steve came home from long journeys wanting nothing more than a pint of beer, a sausage roll and MOTD. I on the other hand would be at the end of a long Saturday parenting our children and be ready for a snuggle and chat. Can you see the problem brewing?

On top of that, if he is asleep, Steve doesn't want to be woken unless the house is on fire, whereas I feel rejected if I'm not kissed goodnight.

It all culminated in one particular evening when Steve came home in the early hours of the morning, snuck into our room to get changed into his PJs, studiously tried not to disturb me and went back downstairs to the trinity of beer, sausage roll and MOTD. I stayed in bed and stewed on how unloved I was and sent him the following message:

"No brownie points for you tonight. You didn't even kiss me!"

Not my finest moment, made worse by his lack of reply and my realisation the following morning that, in my foggy half-asleep state I had actually sent the text to a guy from church.

Obviously, it precipitated a hasty follow-up text to the guy explaining there was no need to kiss me, and he could have all the brownie points he liked if this was never spoken of again.

More importantly, it prompted a conversation between Steve and I about how we'd do late-night returns in the future.

Critically, it helped me to recognise that it was OK for Steve to watch TV downstairs – that it wasn't rejection, it was self-care. That in turn allowed me to think about what I need when I'm exhausted at the end of a long day of parenting, work or managing sick parents. I think one of the healthiest things about our relationship now is recognising that we are each responsible for knowing what empties us of energy and what fills us back up again.

We've learned to communicate our needs better, which helps us love each other well.

But we also understand that what brings each of us joy and recharges our batteries is different, and that part of loving each other well is to respect these differences. I think he probably understood this way before I did. MOTD still doesn't do it for me, instead I just need to go and sit in a room with classical music and a book and let my soul breathe a little. Steve likes to sit

> *We've learned to communicate our needs better, which helps us love each other well.*

and watch quiz shows while his mind resets.

We're so different to one another, but when we communicate well and respect our differences, we make our marriage much stronger.

... one of the healthiest things about our relationship now is recognising that we are each responsible for knowing ourselves, what empties us of energy and what fills us back up again.

Bekah Legg

Bekah Legg is CEO of Restored, a Christian organisation with a mission to speak up about violence against women and equip the church to stand against domestic abuse, and with survivors. She is married to Steve and together they have raised their five fabulous girls and fostered more in a glorious (if sometimes crazy!) blended family.

THE HEART OF MARRIAGE IS ...

making sacrifices

The theory of 'love languages' is an intriguing one. I became aware of it some years ago when I couldn't work out why I was failing to let my wife know just how much I loved her. You see, I'm a man of simple pleasures. Bring me a cup of tea and I get a warm glow inside. In fact, all my wife has to do is add the words "I love you" and that'll keep me happy for months.

Unfortunately, the same doesn't apply to Karen. I tried telling her I loved her every day, but that didn't work. I tried gazing into her eyes while telling her that I loved her, but still no effect. It seemed all the advice I had tried to gain from so-called 'chick flicks' wasn't going to work.

I was at a loss. Until one day I decided to design and lay a new patio. The effect was remarkable. You would've thought I was a cross between St Valentine and Brad Pitt! I had stumbled across my wife's love language – not just 'acts of service' but specifically 'house renovations'.

Thankfully, I found that out over 20 years ago and we are still very happily married, with two daughters, a dog, a cat, goldfish and one surviving chicken.

But here's the rub. I hate DIY and am a totally incompetent handyman. I feel like my brain is being squeezed by a vice every time I have to wield a spanner.

> **"**
>
> *Putting aside our self-interest, desires and needs to see our spouse fulfilled is an incredible journey.*

In other words, it's a sacrifice to do these things, especially in an already busy life.

But what can I do? Doing these things for my wife tells her that I love her. Even though we share the same love language, why it is that all it takes for me is a cuppa but for Karen it's a building project? I don't know. Perhaps whoever designed us this way has a sense of humour.

But our differences point to a greater and much more important truth. Laying down your life for one another is an often-talked-about phrase when it comes to marriage, but on a day-to-day basis, it often looks like just faithfully doing the things that will make your partner feel loved. Karen has made huge sacrifices for me, and I seek to do the same for her. Putting aside our self-interest, desires and needs to see our spouse fulfilled is an incredible journey. When we do that for each other, the surprising end result is a happy, fulfilling and wonderful adventure called marriage.

Carl Beech

Carl Beech is an evangelist, church leader and author who is passionate about reaching out to forgotten people in forgotten places. He is the president of Christian Vision for Men, the leader of Edge Ministries and CEO of Spotlight YOPD, the only UK charity dedicated to young-onset Parkinson's Disease. He has been married to Karen since 1994 and they have two adult daughters.

THE HEART OF MARRIAGE IS ...

finding a better way

One of the most common pieces of relationship advice given to couples is: 'If you want to have a good marriage, then compromise'. But I'm not so sure.

It's not that compromise is a bad thing. Quite the contrary. You need to be able to compromise to successfully navigate any human relationship. But if compromise is the *only* tool we have to help us handle conflict, then we're missing something.

For years, my wife and I relied on compromise to help us get through sticky situations. And none were more sticky than when we tried decorating our house together. We discovered that, although we were deeply in love, we were hopelessly incompatible when it came to interior design. My wife prefers a floral style, but I like minimalism.

I thought I'd scored a major victory when Kate suggested I choose my own preferred scheme for the guest bedroom of our first house. I later discovered how comprehensively I'd been outmanoeuvred when she sweetly pointed out that it was only fair that she now be allowed complete say over our master bedroom. I found myself lying awake, plotting counter-moves, surrounded by an explosion of blossoms, pastels and Laura Ashley prints!

Over the years, decorating our house became a metaphor for negotiating our marriage. We learnt to take turns – you have it your way, then I have it my way. It's the way we managed finances, raised the children, dealt with the in-laws, arranged our social lives etc. Each time, we got to what felt like a fair compromise.

> 66
>
> *... if compromise is the only tool we have to help us handle conflict, then we're missing something.*

But is merely 'fair' what we're aiming for in marriage? At best, it gives a watered-down version of what one party wants; at worst, it allows both parties to go away equally unsatisfied.

The turning point for us came ten years of marriage and two houses later. We started to decorate the bathroom, and one of us had a new idea. How about we try to do this together and combine what we both have, rather than cancelling each other out? And so Floral Minimalism was born!

Synergy is the idea that it's possible to combine different elements into something that's greater than the sum of its parts. It's how the best partnerships work. And it's joyous! I remember Kate and I looking at our finished bathroom and realising that it was quite simply the most stunning room we'd ever worked on together. Not my way or her way, but a third way, a better way – our way.

> 66
>
> **_Synergy is the idea that it's possible to combine different elements into something that's greater than the sum of its parts._**

Ask yourself – what things in your marriage could you do in that third way? What would those fevered discussions about finances, family time, and discipline look like if you pushed beyond compromise and into a creative combination of both your ideas?

We found three keys helpful in making this work:

1. TAKE YOUR TIME
Trying things this way will take more time, so actively cultivate quality time together. Creative solutions are very rarely obvious the first time. There may be a few false starts and you may have to keep persevering through frustration and disagreement. But it's worth the investment.

2. TALK IT THROUGH
Your ability to find synergy is directly related to your ability to communicate well together. You'll be dealing with emotionally charged issues, so it's crucial that you listen, understand where the other is coming from and communicate on a deep level.

3. TRUST EACH OTHER
Finding synergy is like performing a complex dance. You need to trust that your partner won't tread on your toes, stifle your movement or let you fall to the ground. If you have a past history of compromise it at least

demonstrates that you're both willing to put the other first. Try mutual submission, where each of you lays down your own preference in favour of the other's. None of this comes naturally, but it can be developed in every marriage.

So if you want a good marriage, then compromise; but if you want a *great* marriage – find a better way.

> 66
>
> *Finding synergy is like performing a complex dance. You need to trust that your partner won't tread on your toes, stifle your movement or let you fall to the ground.*

Philip Jinadu

Philip leads Woodlands Metro Church in Bristol, part of the Woodlands Church Family, along with his wife, Kate. He is also the founder of the innovative social action initiative, Love Running. Philip and Kate have two adult daughters.

developing a resilient relationship

Mark and I worked out that our marriage was not going to be perfect about five minutes after the ceremony. Our first blazing row took place in the vestry, with both of us fully adorned in our wedding finery! We realised then that staying both married and sane would depend upon our ability to forgive and become stronger throughout the challenges of life.

We all have our share of tests and trials in a long-term relationship. I particularly remember the phase of our lives after Mark and I moved house, changed jobs and had our first baby, all within a few weeks.

Every day seemed to be an emotional roller-coaster, exhausting and full of unexpected twists and turns. I was still coming to terms with being permanently attached to a tiny and mysterious character who apparently had no off switch, while Mark was thrust into a new job with the accompanying stress, joy and a variety of new relationships.

I'll be honest, I envied his interesting life and felt that he had no idea about what was going on in mine. We were digging our own trenches for a while and firing verbal artillery at each other through the tiredness and frustration that we both carried around.

Over more than 20 years of marriage, we have lived through many such phases, albeit featuring different challenges. There have been difficult conversations, tough diagnoses (Mark lost his sight in his twenties) and other challenges that sometimes seemed almost insurmountable. But we have learned some important lessons about resilience along the way.

Resilience is like a muscle that develops as you use it. The truth is you can talk about endurance, you can read books about perseverance, and you can even pray about forgiveness, but until you are willing to personally disarm and deploy these peace-keeping skills amidst the mild skirmish or the long-standing feud, the lines will stay drawn and the battle will continue.

If we want to live in peace and create a stable environment where we will thrive despite difficulty, then we need to intentionally practise these skills. Not only that, but we must work to bounce back and learn from our experiences for the next phase ahead.

And the interesting thing is that after a while, our resilience muscles get stronger. We begin to realise that we can overcome some quite demanding obstacles, and that the person we sometimes treat as our opponent is, in fact, our greatest ally.

We've found that this is the root of a resilient relationship – facing difficult issues together instead of confronting each other. This way, we are much more likely to agree on a solution.

> 66
>
> *We were digging our own trenches for a while and firing verbal artillery at each other through the tiredness and frustration that we both carried around.*

Marriage is not all warfare; far from it. Instead I would say it is a life-long adventure with another unimaginably complex human being. But our ability to negotiate those annoying habits, our determination to resolve conflict and our capacity to stand firm together in the face of disappointment or grief – that is what is at the heart of a resilient relationship.

Developing a resilient relationship

As we commit to building these muscles over time, we will hopefully create a marriage where both partners feel safe, secure and strong as they face the days ahead, for better and for worse, in sickness and in health.

> 66
>
> *And the interesting thing is that after a while, our resilience muscles get stronger. We begin to realise that we can overcome some quite demanding obstacles, and that the person we sometimes treat as our opponent is, in fact, our greatest ally.*

Cathy Madavan

Cathy is a speaker, blogger and author of *Why Less Means More: Making Space for What Matters Most*. She is a regular speaker for Care for the Family, writes for a variety of magazines, and is on the planning team for Spring Harvest. She is married to Mark, a church minister, with whom she has two daughters.

embracing change

During more than 35 years together, we've lived on four continents, been blessed with four children, experienced times of scarcity and relative abundance, and supported each other through both real highs and deep lows.

You'd have thought that we would have learned most of what there was to know about each other in that time, but around 10 years ago we came up against the biggest challenge yet, as we navigated what you might call 'marriage in middle age'.

As strong characters who are quite different from each other, we each brought our share of baggage to the marriage. The adjustments during the early years and when the children arrived were not easy, but we were expecting them.

What we were unprepared for were the mental, physical and psychological changes which middle age brought to us both, changes that were as confusing as they were unexpected. The children were growing up and finances were easing,

... around 10 years ago we came up against the biggest challenge yet, as we navigated what you might call 'marriage in middle age'.

but rather than things becoming easier, we were increasingly irritated with each other.

For several years, we tried talking things through and planned special weekends together to try and re-establish greater harmony. But the arguments intensified and the conflict resolution strategies we had developed over the years no longer worked.

During one supposedly special weekend, we shocked ourselves and each other with the level of anger between us. It was a crunch point which propelled us to seek marriage counselling for a year. For us, this was immensely helpful.

Talking to trusted friends and reading made me realise that what we were experiencing was not unusual. It seems that many couples are unprepared for the complex transitions that are commonly experienced by both men and women in mid-life. This can lead to an isolating perception that you are the only ones facing them.

We discovered that hormone changes affect both men and women. Lower testosterone levels in men can contribute to a desire to slow down, while lower oestrogen and rising testosterone levels in women lead to a greater interest in pursuing challenges outside the home and less willingness to absorb unsatisfactory issues within the relationship.

For us, my husband's career frustrations were a real issue, while friends struggled with empty nest syndrome or found themselves sandwiched between teenagers and ageing parents. Whatever the specifics, there seemed to be stresses from a number of different angles. We both struggled to understand the changes in each other and our relationship, and to provide mutual support while coming to terms with our own significant changes.

We have found it important to approach our male and female 'mid-life crises' as something natural and positive – which is not always how we felt! We both decided (several times) that we did not want to break up, which itself was a powerful incentive to find a constructive way to deal with the changes. It wasn't enough to ignore the issues, be nice to each other and hope things would revert to normal. We needed to re-negotiate some significant issues, including money, time, life and work focus.

We have always aimed for a partnership of equals and this has really helped. We try to love and support each other and face these changes together, drawing on the strength of shared experiences. This means that prioritising regular time together to talk and to do things we both enjoy is every bit as important as it was when we

> *... What we were unprepared for were the mental, physical and psychological changes which middle age brought to us both, changes that were as confusing as they were unexpected.*

Embracing change

were younger – perhaps more so.

Where we hold very different opinions, it's important that we are open to talking about the issues and to approaching some agreement, even if this means respectfully agreeing to differ. We have learned that showing contempt for each other's views within arguments is far more damaging than differences of opinion.

The last 10 years have emphasised for us the commitment involved in facing together the real and continuing changes that building a living relationship involves. But the rewards are worth it and the best is yet to come!

Companionship, trust, mutual commitment and a wealth of shared memories are all important factors in a good marriage. But recognising that our relationship will continue to change – at times significantly – and embracing these changes, however challenging they may seem, is the real heart of marriage.

> 66
>
> *... recognising that our relationship will continue to change – at times significantly – and embracing these changes, however challenging they may seem, is the real heart of marriage*

Janey Lawry-White

Janey is the Chief Operating Officer at Westminster Theological Centre. She has been married to Simon for over 50 years now and they have four adult children and two grandchildren. Together they have lived and worked in Kenya, Malawi, Thailand, the USA and Europe.

THE HEART OF MARRIAGE IS ...

aiming for the best

We so often see couples getting married armed with only a vague hope that their marriage will be one of the ones that will survive. They seem to think it a game of chance, hoping that it doesn't end up in divorce, with the pain and misery that can bring. Instead of continually pursuing a marriage that's the best it can be – strong, rich and fulfilling – they end up going through the motions and live with a marriage that kind of stumbles along in the land of 'OK'.

The trouble with 'OK' is that it can be a dangerous place to be; any slight knock can set it off kilter. And the knocks do come, whether in the form of life circumstances or just a slow, creeping realisation that the person you married isn't perfect.

> 66
>
> *Once we started getting really upset about one difference, we soon began to get upset about others, wondering how on earth we could have married someone so different.*

For my wife and I, the creeping realisation was that we're very different people. It might sound ridiculous, but one of the biggest things we have argued about in our house is tidiness. Contrary to stereotypes, I love things neat and tidy. And Fiona? Well, not so much! She tends to feel life's too short to worry about such things.

It may not seem like a big deal, but there have been times when this little issue has driven a wedge between us. Once we started getting really upset about one difference, we soon began to get upset about others, wondering how on earth we could have married someone so different. And while we were spinning down this track, we forgot we had anything in common.

The thing that has changed this for us has been talking and really trying to understand why these things are so important to each other.

We found that some of our differences are due to our respective upbringings. Not that one was necessarily better than the other, it's just that they were different and caused us to have differing priorities and expectations.

We also started to realise that some of the things that we were now starting to find grating and annoying were the very things that first attracted us to each other. Perhaps I was drawn to Fiona because she had a more 'laid back' approach to life than I did, which I found releasing. And maybe Fiona found that my rather more structured approach to life made hers feel more ordered, stable and secure.

As we stepped into each other's shoes and started to gain understanding, we stopped trying to change each other and instead tried more to change ourselves. So now I don't fret so much about an immaculate house and Fiona has been known to tidy up on occasion!

We've learnt to appreciate these differences too, and understand that they can be positive – we balance each other out and even complement each other. The house isn't so immaculate that people don't feel welcome, but neither is it so untidy it can't be lived in.

Finally, we've learned that we need to always be looking for opportunities to spend time with each other, finding ways to press the 'pause button' and simply hang out with each other. The more we spend quality time together the closer we feel, a bit like when we started dating.

It might sound like things are pretty perfect in our marriage now, right? Actually they aren't. We are great friends, laugh a lot together and have a strong connection.

... we've learned that we need to always be looking for opportunities to spend time with each other, finding ways to press the 'pause button' and simply hang out with each other. The more we spend quality time together the closer we feel, a bit like when we started dating.

But we are also normal people – we argue, we shout occasionally, sometimes we even hurt each other's feelings. But after 30 years of marriage we're more aware than ever of the need to accept and celebrate each other for who we are, and to work together on making our relationship the best it can be.

> 66
>
> *As we stepped into each other's shoes and started to gain understanding, we stopped trying to change each other and instead tried more to change ourselves.*

Andy Banes

Andy and Fiona are joint executive directors of Harmony Consulting, where they lead marriage enrichment weekends. They have two children, a cat, 12 goldfish and four chickens. As well as this, Andy is founder and CEO of a computer software firm. They have been married for 30 years and have two grown-up children.

THE HEART OF MARRIAGE IS ...

choosing 'us'

"So what is at the heart of marriage?" I asked my husband of thirty years, as we walked along a deserted beach in West Wales one January morning. The air was cold, the sky clear and blue, the sand golden, and the waves lapped gently along the shoreline as seagulls circled overhead.

I confess the question was partly prompted by the thought of writing this chapter, but not solely. At that time, not one but two of our children were soon to be tying the knot. In the midst of what I understand is called 'wed-min', I found myself imagining the moment when they would make their vows to each other, promising to be there for the other, whatever the future holds.

"I will love you for better," they say. And the vow replies, "And what of worse?"

"I will love you if we are rich," they say. And the vow enquires, "And if we are poor?"

"I will love you when you are well," they say. And the vow responds, "And in sickness too?"

As a parent I want their marriages to be trouble-free – but I know that's not how it

is. Every marriage has its share of joys and challenges, from without and from within, some welcome and expected, some less so.

Ours has been no exception. There have been moments of laughter, fulfilment and joy – the births of four babies, a new home, new jobs, birthdays and anniversary celebrations. But close on their heels have come times of challenge, disappointment, hurt and pain – from difficulties in the workplace to unrealised dreams, miscommunications, illness and financial pressure.

"I will love you for better," they say. And the vow replies, *"And what of worse?"*

As we walked on the beach, Richard and I reflected that for us, the heart of marriage in both the good times and the bad has been our resolve to approach life not as two individuals but as an 'us'. We haven't always got it right, but seeking to draw closer and face the bad times together, has made the task of pressing through life's challenges more achievable.

And in the good times, having a life companion to share the fun and the joy has made those moments doubly rich and rewarding. It's probably a human reaction for our first thought in any situation to be "What's best for me?" But that little word 'us' is a prompt to step back, to think again and to focus on the shared life we have together. Even when we can't agree, our belief that 'us' is larger than the issue helps us strive to find a way forward together.

These wise words from the ancient book of Ecclesiastes, often read at weddings, describe the strength that comes from approaching life in this way:

"Two are better than one, because they have a good return for their labour. If either of them falls down, one can help the other up. Also, if two lie down together, they will keep warm. But how can one keep warm alone? Though one may be overpowered, two can defend themselves. A cord of three strands is not quickly broken."

While standing together in the good times has been relatively easy, the truth is that we have only been able to face the tough times together by drawing on a strength outside of the confines of our marriage. And we have found this strength in that "cord of three strands" referred to by the author of Ecclesiastes; the two of us drawing on the power and strength that comes from the third strand – our personal faith in God.

It is hard to find a more beautiful description of the contentment that accompanies a belief in a shared future than in Thomas Hardy's novel *Far from the Madding Crowd*, when shepherd Gabriel Oak speaks these words to Bathsheba:

"And at home by the fire, whenever you look up, there I shall be – and whenever I look up, there will be you."

> *We haven't always got it right, but seeking to draw closer and face the bad times together, has made the task of pressing through life's challenges more achievable.*

What a lovely picture of what it means to build a future based on 'us'.

Whether, like our children, you are just embarking on the adventure of marriage, or whether you have 5, 25 or even 50 years of marriage already behind you, it is that shared future, a commitment to 'do life' together – in the good times and the bad – that will see you through.

Katharine Hill

Katharine is the UK Director of Care for the Family and regularly presents marriage and parenting events. As an established author she has written a number of books including *If You Forget Everything Else Remember This – Building a Great Marriage*. Before that, she worked as a solicitor specialising in family law and also served as a magistrate. She and her husband Richard have been married for 39 years and have four children and seven grandchildren.

Further Support

If You Forget Everything Else, Remember This ...
Building a Great Marriage

Covering a range of topics from communicating well, embracing differences, handling in-laws, dealing with financial pressures, and sex and intimacy, Katharine Hill provides wisdom in bite-sized chapters. With real-life stories that will alternately make you laugh and cry, her honest and practical look at marriage is both engaging and encouraging.

cff.org.uk/shop

The Marriage Sessions

The Marriage Sessions is a flexible four-part resource that explores how couples can build a strong relationship. Each session has videos and discussion questions that can be used for a couples' event, or for individual couples to use at home.

cff.org.uk/themarriagesessions

For a range of resources and further support please visit **cff.org.uk/couples**

CareLine

CareLine is a confidential telephone and/or email service which can be accessed by all adults in the UK. Our trusted and caring team will listen and offer support or signposting towards other help as appropriate.

Contact our team Monday to Friday between 9.00am and 4.30pm and say that you would like to speak to a CareLine Advisor:
mail@cff.org.uk | 029 2081 0800